Revising

CW00819147

by
Colin Buchanan
Bishop of Aston

GROVE BOOKS LIMITED
Bramcote   Nottingham   NG9 3DS

CONTENTS

First Impression January 1989

ISSN 0144-1728
ISBN 1 85174 103 8

INTRODUCTION

It is ten years this year since the touching up of the texts to go into the ASB reached its final climax in General Synod. It is nearly nine years since Rite A went into use, and well over eight since the whole ASB came on to market. This means that Rite A in particular has now had a longer stable period of shopwindow use than any of the eucharistic rites in Series 1, 2, or 3 had in the years from 1966 to 1980. And with both Series 2 and Series 3 even four years' usage had two simultaneous and opposite effects: firstly, to entrench the notion that this particular rite, for all its appearance of being a newcomer, was in fact to many people the Anglican tradition (and therefore not to be touched by would-be amenders); and, secondly, to expose those weaknesses in a rite which only sustained use can show—in other words, to show where the ribs are sticking out. Both these effects are further re-inforced by both the continuous eight years of usage of the ASB, and by its hard covers and substantial bulk (and corresponding cost), which, in contrast with little booklets, advertise this Book's apparent permanence. Both effects point to the same remedy—that is, that we should do our utmost to prepare for change. For liturgy nowadays is bound to have the flexibility which is demanded by changing times, contexts, and attitudes; and minds should be prepared for that, rather than being lulled into a sense of a 'tradition' which, it is supposed, will run on forever just because it is tradition. Equally, if deficiencies are being exposed in the text and the other provisions of a rite, then we owe to ourselves and our successors not just to prepare for change, but to prepare changes.

That is what this Booklet is addressing. We are far on in the life of the new Liturgical Commission which was appointed in 1986. First signs of its work have appeared, and more is about to break surface. I attempt here to engage with the ASB provision in a way which is supportive to the work of the Commission (and, indeed, of the House of Bishops and of the General Synod)—and the present Commission has, of course, no necessary stakes in the contents of the ASB which took shape from their point of view almost during Anglican liturgical pre-history.

I have always resisted the older notion (which prevailed in my student days and when I answered the General Ordination Examination), that the authorized texts are a virtually exhaustive view of Anglican worship. Such a view is manifestly unsustainable, and is generally abandoned.[1] There is therefore always a need for coaching materials, helps to leaders of worship and to participants in worship to ensure that they take maximum

[1] When I was ordained, to know the BCP text was, for examination purposes at least, to know the Church of England's worship! I have written more fully on this general point (though in connection with hymnody and music) in a recent article 'Music in the context of Anglican Liturgy' in Robin Sheldon (ed.) *In Spirit and In Truth* (Hodder and Stoughton, 1989).

advantage of the rites on offer.[1] But, although I commend such enterprises, and sometimes join the coaching, this Booklet is not in that category. This is instead an attempt to address the question: should there be something else on offer?

This is a relatively short-term programme. I apologize to readers from other countries and other denominations, for it bears directly only upon the Church of England. [2] Even there, whilst it may help lay foundations for beyond 2000, it is distinctly the coming decade which is in view. It is not particularly visionary. It is not *The Future of Anglican Worship*.[3] It is perhaps nearer to *Towards Liturgy 2000*.[4] It is what could, and arguably should, be done right now.

That does not mean that how materials are used is irrelevant to this particular exploration. In days when the Charismatic (or 'renewal') Movement on the one hand, and the logic of the 'domesticating' implications of the Liturgical Movement on the other, have loosened us all up, there are strong textual implications. The needs of the times are not met simply by alternating a minimal number of fixed texts interspersed with widely permissive rubrics, nor are they met simply by publishing poker-faced texts which are then undercut by the explosive force of the coaching in their own 'pastoral introductions'. Somehow the programme must have an integrity which serves the liturgical needs of the times, but is at peace with itself, and emerges reasonably comfortably from the ASB and its usage currently to be found.

---

[1] The general run of this Grove Worship Series is designed *exactly* to provide such coaching.

[2] I have tried, in a superficial way, to address international Anglicanism in my recent *Lambeth and Liturgy 1988* (Grove Worship Series 106, 1989)—and both categories get a little attention in my monthly *News of Liturgy*.

[3] Trevor Lloyd (compiler) *The Future of Anglican Worship* (Grove Worship Series 100, Grove Books, 1987). This does attempt to be visionary—it was the Group for Renewal of Worship marking its 'ton'.

[4] This is the title of a symposium edited by Michael Perham, advertised by the SPCK, London, at the point this Booklet goes to press. As the blurb issued by the publishers says that the contributors will argue that 'the ASB is wearing thin' its aim stands near to that of this Booklet. But I have not seen its contents, and suspect that their chapters will have reached their final state before they have seen this.

1. BACKGROUND

The ASB was authorized in November 1979 for a ten-year period of life from 10 November 1980 to 31 December 1990.[1] As a Book it had certain clear characteristics:

(a) It was in modern English—at least to the point of commonly 'addressing God as "you"'.

(b) It was 'alternative'—in other words, 1662 remained unchanged as the 'basic' worship book of the Church of England, though the law permitted every parish to choose whether or not to use ancient or 'modern services.

(c) Largely it covered the same liturgical ground of rites and sacraments as the old Book, as it was in those areas that synodical action had to be taken to get services authorized.[2]

(d) Nevertheless, its theology was more related to the realities of English society than 1662 appears to be to-day. [3] The people of God have ceased to be co-terminous with the English nation, and thus the unity and 'bonding' of the church as the body of Christ have become far more highlighted, as the church recognizes its divine calling not only to holiness in discipleship, but also to a missionary and ethical confrontation with a 'world' outside of 'the church.

(e) Thus in turn the provision of the ASB is for pastoral liturgy, consistent enough to be recognizable in every parish where it is in use, but flexible enough to be used to meet the needs of this congregation, with these resources, in this building.

(f) The pastoral character of the liturgy is re-inforced by its highly participatory role for the congregation.

(g) All the major sacramental and quasi-sacramental rites of the 1662 Book have in fact, for a combination of scholarly and pastoral reasons, been structurally altered so that each now exhibits a different groundplan from that in 1662.[4]

[1] For details of the authorization see my *Latest Liturgical Revision in the Church of England 1978-1984* (Grove Liturgical Study 39, 1984).
[2] It was arguable that Thanksgiving for the Birth of a Child (or for Adoption) and one or two small other items feel outside the provisions of 'alternative' services, but the small nature of such exceptions proves the general point. See also footnote 2 on p.9 below.
[3] At the time of writing I am engaged in a public controversy about the nature and desirability of the state establishment of the Church of England. On this point, as a good instance, 1662 equates the nation with the people of God, whereas the ASB knows that there is a small gathered company of believers with a mission from their gathering for worship into an unbelieving society around. It is a fundamental distinction. See also footnote 1 on p.12 below.
[4] This is not true, of course, of daily offices, and in some other cases the traditional structure can still be followed as one option on offer.

Such was the Book launched on the Church of England in November 1980. It has passed into very wide popular use, and in many places has long since driven out (by popular consent) the ancient Cranmerian forms. We thus have now both adult converts, and young people who grew up in Anglican parishes in the nineteen-seventies (when modern language booklets came into use) and the nineteen-eighties (when the ASB has been current), who have never known what it is to worship with the uses of 1662, and who have never thought to miss them. The ASB has become the *de facto* norm of liturgical texts across the land of England.

During the first six years of life of the ASB various other liturgical forms deriving from the Liturgical Commission were also authorized in the Church of England. There were some residual Series 1,2 and 3 Booklets.[1] There was *Ministry to the Sick* in 1983. There was *Lent Holy Week Easter,* commended by the House of Bishops, and published in January 1986. There was a small Booklet *Prayer and Dedication after a Civil Marriage,* commended in the same way, and published later that year. But there was also an awareness that the ten years authorized life of the ASB would run out in 1990, and urgent action would be needed in the quinquennium 1985-1990 to provide a policy (and possibly texts) for the years beyond 1990.

It was with this in view that I was asked by the Liturgical Commission in Winter 1984-5 to draft a forward-looking document on policy. My draft drew attention to the shifting scene of the coming years: in the evaluation of the ASB in actual use, in language, in doctrinal emphases, in ecumenical needs, in the sharpening of the Church's mission. This draft of mine, for reasons beyond anyone's control, was never discussed by the Liturgical Commission before it was hi-jacked by the Standing Committee of General Synod, and issued as a Standing Committee document, *The Worship of the Church* (GS 698), in time for the first session of the General Synod newly elected in September 1985.

Lo and behold, my draft had suffered a sea-change. Whilst the bulk of the review of the current situation remained virtually untouched, the practical application at the end of the report had now taken a U-turn. Instead of looking forward, it looked fairly stolidly back. My draft had not envisaged that the ASB could be superseded by 1990, and had therefore recommended that a further five year period of authorization should be considered towards the end of the 1980s. Despite all the evidence of a rolling and fluid situation, the report as published ended with a triumphant statement of policy—that there should be a review of ASB, and there should be provision of new materials to supplement and enrich it—and therefore 'the Synod is asked to remove the uncertainty about the future of the ASB 1980 by extending its period of authorization, not indefinitely...but for a second period of ten years.'[2] Thus the first two sessions of the newly elected Synod were asked on the spot to give this extended authorization to the ASB, and the Synod duly did so (the main mutters against it coming

---

[1] Most lapsed at the end of 1985. Series 1 Marriage and Funeral rites, and Series 2 Baptism and Confirmation rites, had their authorization renewed until 31 December 1990.
[2] *The Worship of the Church,* p.23.

from the Prayer Book lobby—a species *redivivus* in that Synod—such that those who looked prophetically forward found themselves driven to defending the ASB, rather than superseding it). It somehow became a bold and positive move to affirm so far in advance the continued usefulness of an unchanged ASB right up to the eve of the next century. The Report said that great change was coming and inevitably must be taken into account, and therefore we must remove uncertainty by voting for no change—and the Synod bought it.

In the Spring of 1986 a new Commission was announced, under a new chairman, Bishop Colin James of Winchester. This Commission has been very hard at work, and has neither tried nor wished to be free of all leaks.[1] There is evidence that they have taken the forward-looking parts of *The Worship of the Church* agenda extremely seriously.[2] They have also been very conscious of the recommendations of *Faith in the City*.[3] And they have reached their own discernment that the Church of England could do with a new dollop of special seasonal provision for 'All Saints to Candlemas'. Nevertheless at the time of writing very little of their work has officially broken surface in published form—the sole products of 1988 being an amazingly archaeological-looking pamphlet on *The Liturgical Ministry of Deacons*[4], and a far more important document at the end of the year, *Making Women Visible*.[5]

Many of the matters with which the new Commission has to wrestle are set out item by item in the chapters below, and are the subject of my own,

---

[1] At the time of writing, whilst little has yet been published that would tell us what they were doing, this admirable policy of contrived leakiness is helping spread the message aright—leaks come from meetings of the Commission with diocesan liturgical secretaries, from the minutes of the House of Bishops (which refer to the titles of documents submitted, even when the contents of them are unknown), and from a deliberately non-secretive style among the members.

[2] These include the concept of a 'directory', the principle of 'inclusive language', and the provision for ecumenical needs. Of course the 1986 Liturgical Commission did not come as strangers to The Worship of the Church—there were several key members in common between the Commission which (nearly!) produced the Report and the new Commission which was to act on it.

[3] Cf. Recommendation 19: 'The Liturgical Commission should pay close attention to the liturgical needs of Churches in the urban priority areas.' (*Faith in the City: The Report of the Archbishop of Canterbury's Commission on Urban Priority Areas* (Church House Publishing, 1985) p.362). This report was published just too late to affect *The Worship of the Church* in any direct way, though (insofar as *Faith in the City* touches on worship at all) the thrust of the ACUPA report can be brought relatively easily within the forward-looking provision of the argument about strategy in *The Worship of the Church*.

[4] Cf. 'Deacons are at the point of appropriation and interchange, and symbolize in their movement between the people and the altar the union of the whole worshipping community: the deacon is the go-between.' (*The Liturgical Ministry of Deacons* (GS Misc 291) p.7)

[5] The very month of publication of this—January 1989—the House of Bishops has been considering the following documents originating from (or near) the Liturgical Commission:
'Code of Practice' for the implementation of the Ecumenical Canons
'Reaffirmation of Baptism'
'Funeral Service for a Child Dying near the Time of Birth'
'Ministry and the Time of Death'
'Proposals for Liturgy in UPAs and for Family Services'
Some of these are for immediate publication, some for reconsideration by the Liturgical Commission. *Making Women Visible* itself will shortly become a published document, depending on the debate in General Synod as this goes to press.

strictly unofficial and certainly uninspired, comment. And, whilst the terms of reference from the House of Bishops in 1986 are the main charter under which the Commission works, a new factor has arisen through the Anglican Consultative Council's meeting in 1987, and the Lambeth Conference of 1988. Both these bodies have been reflecting upon ways in which a common international 'Anglicanism' in liturgy could be discerned or encouraged—partly with a view to strengthening the bonds of the Anglican Communion. The ACC proposed an International Liturgical Commission, but this idea was resisted by the second International Anglican Liturgical Consultation, meeting at Brixen, Northern Italy, in August 1987.[1] The meeting of the ACC Standing Committee did not proceed with this Commission notion. Meanwhile at the Lambeth Conference in Summer 1988, a plenary resolution had called for the Primates to set up an international 'Advisory Body' which would monitor liturgical developments and keep a unity of doctrinal stance to it.[2] This Body is also very unlikely to come into existence. Thus, although there is some uncoordinated concern lest 'inculturation' of the liturgy lead to too great a fragmentation as between parts of the Anglican worlds, it is clear that the autonomy and independence of each Province is secured.

[1] The ACC proposals are to be found in *Many Gifts One Spirit: Report of ACC-7* (Church House Publishing for ACC, 1987) pp.74-76. The 'Brixen Submission' has only appeared in print in *News of Liturgy* for August 1987, though copies were made available to certain working groups at the Lambeth Conference.

[2] See Lambeth Resolution 18 (6), and my own commentary on it in *Lambeth and Liturgy 1988* (Grove Worship Series 106, 1989), pp.24-25.

2. SCOPE AND LIMITATIONS

Whilst the form and contents of the ASB are nowadays taken for granted, there is a mixture of the inevitable and the accidental within it. From one point of view, its starting point is the provision in the Church of England (Worship and Doctrine) Measure 1974 that services 'alternative' to those in the BCP could be authorized by vote of Synod, and only by that route. This invested the synodical process with a determinative weight in the compiling of the ASB. There were some decisions taken which were not synodical, but the broad sweep of contents was the outcome of synodical processes.[2] All 'alternative' services had to go down the synodical route, and this both concentrated that group of rites together on the one hand, and virtually squeezed other categories of rites out of consideration on the other.[1] As a general rule, the pressures of time, the difficulties of reaching wide agreement in some sensitive areas, and the lack of a sense of need for offical provision in most other areas, all conspired together to produce a Book which would provide a backbone of liturgical texts for a decade ahead for the central rites of the Church of England, but without very much creative responding to all the actual needs there are.

Another limitation of the ASB lay in its relatively untried state at the point of authorization. The degree of this lack of trial certainly varied for instance, Rite A, which went through a full revision process in General Synod, benefitted greatly from five years use of Series 3 Communion. But Series 3 baptism and confirmation services only came into use in Summer 1979, and were immediately 'adapted' (without fullscale revision) to take their place in the ASB. They benefitted, no doubt, from Series 2 initiation services, which had been in use for over ten years before Series 3 arrived. But in general, as these services illustrate, rites were still written by the Commission, revised by the Synod, and then authorized and brought into use on the back of all too little live usage. It is thus inevitable that there should be many point of infelicity of wording, of bathos, or of clumsiness, which went through the screening without being spotted. After four years use of Series 2 services in the early seventies we reckoned that the ribs were showing at certain points—and although the ASB had all the Series 2 and Series 3 use behind it, eight years use of it has predictably found out its weak spots also.

However, a greater spur to change comes through the limitations imposed by history. The ASB was conceived, gestated, and delivered all in the 1970s. That decade was its formative period—now we face the

---

[1] 'Non-synodical' decisions covered: the inclusion of some BCP texts; the choice of versions of the scriptures for passages set out in extenso; and type-face, arrangement, and sequence of liturgical texts.

[2] Two rites which did not need authorization as alternative services, but nevertheless received it, were 'Thanksgiving after the Birth of a Child' and 'Thanksgiving after Adoption'. These were included in the single package of 'Initiation Services', and thus came in though they are self-evidently not alternative to anything in the BCP.

1990s. And the following limitations of history are built into its provisions:

(a) The 1970s were still in a state of deference to the BCP tradition. That does not necessarily mean that we should now abolish the Collect for Purity or Cranmer's Prayer of Humble Access. But we should be free to consider these and comparable changes, which in the 1970s were unthinkable. The very presence of Rite B in the ASB is another facet of this deference; the structure of daily offices is another; and perhaps the form of Rite A 'following the pattern of the Book of Common Prayer' is another

(b) In the 1970s the whole thrust of the exercise was towards having a single book.[1] In the 1980s the concept was well breached, and may now be viewed as dead or dying.[2] Thus the field is wide open for new exploration of the kinds of book (if any) that we need in the 1990s.

(c) *Faith in the City* was not yet in view in the 1970s, and its liturgical agenda were not well envisaged in official liturgical drafting.[3] It is clear that the present Liturgical Commission envisages the use of a 'Directory'—a far more flexible provision of liturgical 'units' (perhaps even to be understood as 'liturgical building blocks') than has ever been known officially before. If this principle were to be taken seriously, then (one assumes) liturgical revision would become like cleaning the windows of Buckingham Palace—it would just go on and on, in a small way, all the time, and never be attempted in a single all-in crash programme.

(d) 'Inclusive language', though known from the North American examples, was no part of official policy, and did not become so until 1983.[4] This means that, from the historical point of view, the ASB could

---

[1] The issue was initially debated in these terms, and, once the general decision had been taken in February 1976, all the synodical energies were bent towards getting the contents ready for the one Book for November 1979, when the final votes on those contents were taken.

[2] In the first quinquennium after 1980, we had *Ministry to the Sick* (authorized as strictly 'alternative' to rites in the BCP); we also considered, but rejected, The Blessing of Oils and A Form for the Reconciliation of a Penitent also as 'alternatives'. We then had *Lent Holy Week Easter* and *A Form of Prayer and Dedication to be used after a Civil Marriage*—neither of which was 'alternative' but instead was 'commended' by the House of Bishops. There have been no plans to collect these rites into a single monster Book—and, if we pick up the hints of what is come, as, e.g. a 'Directory' (see paragraph (c) below), then we can see that the ASB will soon look quite selective in what it includes and excludes.

[3] See p.7 above, also the treatment of 'Simplicity of Language' in (MM) Paragraph 189 of the Lambeth Conference Report *The Truth Shall Make You Free* (Church House Publishing, 1989) p.69) and the warnings about 'book culture' in Paragraph 190 immediately following it.

[4] In other words, the drafting of *Lent Holy Week Easter*, which started to take serious shape that year, was the first creative writing done by the Commission on the 'inclusivity' principle. It was not loudly advertised, and many may have used the rites without spotting the principle!

hardly have been produced at a worse time. We now have the spectacle of the Commission presenting a far-reaching report, Making Women Visible, which would, in effect change the whole text of the ASB, but cannot actually be dubbed into it, but can only be 'commended' as viable under Canon B.5.[1] We have already reached the point of considerable uncertainty as to what texts will be followed (i.e. the printed one or a variant) on any particular occasion—how it would feel ten years from now, if the official ASB remained, is anybody's guess.

(e) The ASB was restricted initially by the lack of official Versions of the Bible approved by the Synod for inclusion in official texts. Thus the readings set out in extenso were drawn simply from the RSV, the Jerusalem Bible (JB), the NEB, and To-Day's English Version (TEV). Not only so—the NEB was laid far too heavily under contribution from among those four; and in any case the choice of versions generally might well not stand up to close inspection.[2] Since 1980 the New International Version (NIV) has passed into far more widespread use, and the JB and the NEB have been revised. In my opinion, the NIV is the version most likely not only to provide a fair modern translation within the 'family' of the Great English Bible, the AV, the RV, and the RSV, but also to leave worshippers generally with the 'feel' that this is the text of the English Bible which can be learned and trusted to-day.

(f) A further historical development has come through the creation, approval, and authorization of the Church of England (Ecumenical Relations) Measure 1988, which ushers in the two new Ecumenical Canons, B43 and B44, both due to be promulged on 30 January 1989, as this Booklet is published. Whilst B43 hardly touches the texts which can count as Anglican, or at least as approved by the Church of England for its members to use, B44 opens a whole range of new textual possibilities. The purpose of B44 is to over-rule the Church of England's general rules on worship in those congregations and areas where a merging or sharing of worshipping life with non-Anglicans is occurring.[3] In place of the canonical forms of worship the diocesan bishop may write tailor made rules for each particular Local Ecumenical Project. At the time of writing the House of Bishops is commending a Code of Practice which will guide such usage. The Liturgical Commission has been involved in drafting the Code, and in the process has had to think hard about the kinds of liturgical provision which will be needed, partly for services like joint confirmations, partly for ordinary regular Sunday use.

[1] Making Women Visible: The Use of Inclusive Language with the ASB (Church House Publishing, 1989).

[2] One of my happiest memories of liturgical revision was sitting with chosen New Testament passages open before me both in Greek and in the four English versions from which we were selecting. The passages had to be read for accuracy of translation and for ease of reading aloud, and the study was fruitful for me, if not for those who follow my recommendations (but in any case I only worked on a few Sundays of the year). The opening and post-communion sentences are not always from a known version, whilst the 'Liturgical Psalter' had its own separate 'canonization' as a version of the Bible'.

[3] I have written a coaching manual on B44 (with the text of the Canon in it)—No. 101 in this Series, Anglicans and Worship in Local Ecumenical Projects (Grove Books, 1987).

(g) There is a severe limitation on the scope of the ASB through its severe 'textuality'. I said at the outset that there is great need for coaching provision as to how to use official materials well. It is at least arguable that such coaching should be officially part of the authorized rites, and not some unofficial gloss upon them. One of the strengths of *Lent Holy Week Easter* is that, being only 'commended', and thus not having to undergo a tight synodical passage, it presents introductory material with the liturgical texts. The opening 'Notes', which began with Series 3 communion in 1973, were a half-step in the right direction. But the next step would require, at the beginning of each published rite, prose advice about its use, of a sort which General Synod could conceivably itself commend, but could hardly amend, line by line and comma by comma. The *Lent Holy Week Easter* provision evaded the Synod and thus kept the Commission's coaching, but could anything deemed 'alternative', and thus seeking full authorization, fare similarly? The same would apply to the principle, in many ways to be applauded, of attaching devotional material to the liturgical texts, or of writing hints about personal devotion and spirituality into any introductions. Perhaps we should also look forward to a further fulfilment of the Commission's terms of reference by their providing other back-up material (whether it goes through the Synod or not) which is directed to the areas of training and 'liturgical formation'— that is, materials which are person-orientated as much as programme-orientated.

(h) Another limitation, if it may be so described, upon the ASB is the great rash of creative liturgical writing in other parts of the Anglican Communion *since* it was completed—in other words, contemporary liturgical resources to which the compilers of the ASB had by definition no access during its gestation period. Now the rites of, say, New Zealand and Canada, and the 'inculturated' new eucharistic rite in Kenya, and other drafting elsewhere (there are forward-looking hints, for instance, in Scotland and South Africa) all challenge the worn ASB tradition with some sparkling and meritorious alternative drafting.

(i) Finally, the mission situation in England continues to clarify itself. Less and less is the Church of England to be identified with the nation at prayer. The idea has been incredible since 1689 anyway, but has still apparently been believed into living memory. Rite A itself exhibits a strong contrast with 1662 at just this point—that is, that the text is that of a gathered Christian community, acknowledging and strengthening the unity in Christ of its members who attend, and then sending them back into an unbelieving world, there to witness to Christ and to pursue his mission. The times move on again, and the ASB itself needs to come under scrutiny from this standpoint. There are implications, of course, for the parliamentary 'establishment' of the Church of England.[1] But there are also strong implications for the Church of England's self-understanding, and that in turn affects our expression in liturgy.

[1] Whilst writing these lines, I have found myself pitchforked into some extraordinary publicity on just this issue. I draw attention to a full discussion ('Mission and Establishment') I wrote for the pre-Lambeth book, P.Turner and F. Sugano (eds.) *Crossroads are for Meeting* (SPCK, USA, 1986, distributed in Britain by Grove Books). See also *The Future of Anglican Worship* (Grove Worship Series 100, 1987) pp.18-19, and a passing warning in the 1988 Lambeth Conference Report, *The Truth Shall Make You Free*, p.84.

3. CALENDAR AND LECTIONARY

The Calendar is the foundational feature of the lectionary provision—no lectionary can be compiled until its calendrical frame is known, and discussions of competing lectionaries in fact always drive the proponents back to calendars. The ASB calendar had its own innovatory features—notably the nine Sundays before Christmas, with the implication of the church year starting in October. Whilst it has had some impact on other Churches, through its own ecumemical origins in the Joint Liturgical Group and through its adoption in other Anglican Churches (as, e.g. in the Church of Ireland's Alternative Prayer Book (1984)), yet, on a world scene, it still has only a small foothold in a territory still occupied by the traditional calendar. This traditional calendar, which begins the church year in Advent, has been much reinforced by the creation of modern lectionaries (notably the Roman Catholic one) to fit the inherited calendrical base.[1] The Church of England itself remains technically committed to the BCP calendar, to which the ASB is only an 'alternative', and the clash of two calendars can provide problems in use.

There are many merits in the ASB pattern, and the lectionary provision which fits it has many advantages over the Roman Catholic three-year Sunday lectionary. In particular the thematic treatment of each Sunday should, in my opinion, stand. Indeed, it is arguable that what the provisions really need is a critical toothcombing, and then, if necessary, a re-creation on the two-year basis. There are already ten Sundays in the list which have different themes for each of the two years, and careful work over the Sundays from Pentecost 6 onwards (which currently have the same theme for each of two years) might expand the scope of scriptural teaching available.

At the time of writing, we also have a new set of draft proposals from the Liturgical Commission being aired. The Commission, after several public hints, introduced draft materials for a 'season' from All Saints Day to Candlemas to a consultation of diocesan liturgical secretaries in November. In the draft forms they have accepted the pre-Christmas celebration of Christmas, have by a knock-on process written Advent themes into the Sundays prior to Advent (thus dispensing with the current Old Testament themes), and have moved Bible Sunday out of the nine altogether. Whilst the ideas thus formulated are no more than ideas, and will certainly get plenty of airing before ever being adopted, a conservative response is bound to ask whether thus fiddling with the pre-Christmas Sundays does

[1] There was a debate in General Synod in 1984 about the relative merits of the ASB and the Roman Catholic Lectionaries, and at the end of it the Synod declined to give the latter any official authorization. Whilst Anglicans in other parts of the world (and the Lambeth Conferences of 1978 and 1988) have in various ways put confidence in the Roman Catholic Lectionary (sometimes, in an adapted form, called the 'Common Lectionary'), it looks improbable that it could qualify as the answer to all our Church of England needs in the near future.

not in the process upset the balance of the whole year's provision. There is of course a kind of precedent in the special alternative lectionary of Holy Week provided in the official services, but that bolsters the Holy Week themes without disturbing any other balance. From the sound of it, the new proposals could seriously affect the totality of the year.

There is a new 'spirit in the air' about lectionaries, however, and there are signs that it is getting to the Commission. In essence, the mood is to allow the wholeness of the scriptural text to speak for itself more: by continuous reading (something much to be desired in the Epistles), by permission for longer passages of, say, Old Testament narrative, and by encouragement of dialogue and dramatic reading, of which the Passion Gospels are a good archetype.[1]

Re-touching the whole calendar and lectionary provision also entails a hard look at the following random agenda items:

(a) should collects be written round themes? [2]

(b) could psalmody be more 'theme-related'?

(c) is there any point in taking fancy snippets from the Old Testament for Saints' Days? Should non-biblical passages about the saints concerned—where anything is known—be provided or permitted?

(d) how are we to pick the lesser holy day candidates? The Lambeth Conference has asked for an international 'process'.[3] The Church of England's experience suggests great frustration with votes in the House of Bishops and on the floor of the Synod.[4] Equally, it is not at all clear that sheer 'emergence' from the local scene is sufficient.

(e) can one last heave be made to obtain a fixed Easter?

---

[1] Cf. the discussion in the recent Joint Liturgical Group publication, Donald Gray (ed.) *The Word in Season: The Use of the Bible in Liturgy* (Canterbury Press, 1988).

[2] One tintack worth noting is the phrase 'the Virgin Mary, full of grace', in the Advent 4 Collect. Whilst the petition that follows asks that God would 'fill us' with grace (which is orthodox!), the implication of 'plena gratia' seems far too obviously to be about Mary as a fountain of grace.

[3] Resolution 60, *The Truth Shall Make You Free*, p.236. See also my comments in *Lambeth and Liturgy 1988*, p.25.

[4] It must not be forgotten that 15 August ('St. Mary's Day') was moved to 8 September on a snap vote in Synod simply to make it relate better to holidays—whilst Josephine Butler, having been introduced at Revision Stage on the floor of the House, was defeated in Synod by 120 votes to 117, and then reinstated in the House of Bishops by 22 votes to 21—the good woman had become a football.

4. NON-SACRAMENTAL WORSHIP

Daily Offices

The ASB provides both a longer and a shorter form of daily offices. There is a half-spoken expectation that the shorter form provides for individuals or small groups—perhaps often a parish staff—to have a framework for daily prayer and Bible reading. The problem the form throws up is that of sameness, and, whilst the strength of an office is in its relative predictability and 'safeness' (as well as its actual provision), there are models around the Anglican world which suggest a greater of materials. *An Australian Prayer Book* (1978) has won much applause for what is in effect a different office for each morning and evening for each of the six week-days. Thus each morning and each evening of the week has its own 'office Psalm', its own office collect (used in one of two places), its own office Canticle (as our Shorter form has), and its own distinctive suggestions for a pattern of intercessions and thanksgivings. It has proved itself as a breakfast-table office as well as as a church or clergy-study one. The *Canadian Book of Alternative Services* (1985) is not so adventurous but it offers a penitential rite, a mid-day office, and a 'Service of Light' over and above the basic offices; it also has a 'Vigil of the Resurrection' for Saturday nights, and a marvellous range of canticles (with seasonal re-allocations), and of responsive materials—so rich and extensive indeed as almost to recall the Rules called the Pie. Regular users would find much to add an ordered variety to daily offices, if they work at it. The newly authorized *A New Zealand Prayer Book* (1989) has over 150 pages of text for offices, and it includes basic offices (following the traditional plan), but in addition there are: 'Daily Services' with separate provision of canticles and prayers for each morning and evening of the week; additional 'songs of praise' (i.e. canticles), such as 'The Desert shall Blossom' (Is.35); a further distinct programme for 'Daily Devotions', providing what is nearer to a 'lay office' (a great need in England), centring on reflection on Gospel or Epistle; supplementary prayers with index; an astonishingly flexible mid-day office; night prayers (once called 'Compline'); and 'family prayers'. We should begin a dialogue between these three samples and ASB usage. The only moves in that direction so far are the penitential material and the night prayers from *Lent Holy Week Easter.* A thorough dialogue would also raise questions about the appropriate quantity of psalmody, and its theological purpose in an office.

Sunday Offices

Where traditional Morning and Evening Prayer survive for Sunday use today, even if ASB forms are used rather than 1662 ones, yet the rite tends to run coolly and predictably, and may not be subject to the same criticisms as it is in its daily use. Congregations which wish to abandon Sunday offices do so very cheerfully, and do not feel constrained to use it.[1]

What may be needed for Sundays is a closer awareness of the lectionary themes. If the 'prime' scriptural readings are allocated to the eucharist, then, if there is no eucharist (or only a hole-in-a-corner one), then those

---

[1] Are they allowed to dispense with Morning and Evening Prayer on Sundays? The answer from Canon B.11(2) of the Canons of the Church of England is: only after the bishop has made enquiry and is satisfied and gives dispensation. Of course, some clergy may provide these offices at unsociable hours, but the likelihood in parish communion parishes is that the offices have usually ceased. The bearing of this upon family services (as discussed lower down in this chapter) is also interesting.

prime readings ought to be earmarked for the chief service of the day, and not simply be passed by. This in turn provokes the thought, which had a flurry of publicity in the late 1960s and has recently returned to stimulate us again, that a non-sacramental service of a gathered Sunday sort of event might well be a variant on ante-communion, rather than a descendant of Cranmer's Morning or Evening Prayer.[1]

Other Sunday Services

Out beyond those rites which might by a stretch be called 'Sunday Offices' there are other patterns both in use and in gestation at the moment. The popular public service is the 'Family Service', by which most parishes at the evangelical end of the Anglican spectrum mean a non-sacramental, and relatively non-formal, service of the word. The genre rose well above the ideas of any one parish way back in the 1960s, when the Eclectics (a national younger clergy society) produced their own favoured pettern, and it was disseminated through the CPAS book *Family Worship* (1971), and has since been updated and enriched, until it takes its latest shape in *Church Family Worship,* a hard-back A5 book of around 300 pages with a strong seasonal and thematic flavour (Hodder and Stoughton, 1986).

The bishops of the Church of England have over many years found these family services disconcerting and even slightly infuriating. This may arise partly from the actual churchmanship of the bishops but it also stemmed from the apparent thin-ness liturgically of the rites at which they sometimes found themselves present.[2] This in turn has led to calls for better models to be used—though it is self-evident that, if a parish is using a non-sacramental family service not as a statutory service, but as something outside of the reach of authorization altogether, then the use concerned will not be amenable to reform 'from above' (whether by Commission, Synod, or bishop). The most official bodies of the Church of England can do is to advise family service parishes how on their own terms they can do better. That does not mean the Commission should not be working at good models; clearly they should be, and certainly they are. But it does mean that such models will only have a lightweight status (perhaps as 'Commended by the House of Bishops') once published, and will bind no-one and have little claim for inclusion in books of official services.

All-Age Teaching Patterns

Whilst the 'All-Age Sunday School' is associated in English minds more with American Baptists and Presbyterians than with the parish church on the corner, there are here too patterns to explore, which may have little structural relationship to the offical services. We can do no more here than drop a hint.[3]

[1] Cf. Methodist provision in *The Methodist Service Book* (1975).
[2] In the contrast a bishop may have experienced between a well-ordered eucharist liturgy in one parish and an untidy and perhaps liturgically thinner non-sacramental service in another, then it is clear which gets the immediate palm. If we stand back from appearances, however, it is always at least possible that the participants in the family service would not have been in church at all in the other parish—and then the comparison becomes complex. A family service usually is an element in a policy of outreach in an evangelistic parish, whereas a eucharist have a different ideology behind it.
[3] Two reported instances of such exploratory patterns in English parishes are: at Trinity St. Michael, Wealdstone, Harrow (see Trevor Lloyd, *Introducing Liturgical Change* (Grove Worship Series 87, 1984)) and at St. George's, Leeds (see Judith Rose, *Sunday Learning for All Ages* (Grove Pastoral Series 11, 1982)). Each should be checked against current practice at the time of reading.

5. HOLY COMMUNION

The communion service stands at the centre of a Church's liturgical programme, and the text and rubrics include an element of public proclamation of a Church's doctrinal stance. Rite A has certainly acquired that 'normative' role.[1] How should it properly be moved forward?

Clearly the point of need which accords most closely with ground already covered is that of flexibility. The general ethos of the rite already tends that way, and creative planning and leadership can, for instance, already legally provide home-grown (or borrowed) material for an opening sentence of scripture, for penitence, for intercessions, for the lead-in to the Peace, for additional words of invitation to communion, for a post-communion sentence, and for post-communion prayers. In matters of music, hymnody, vesture, ceremonial, decor, and lay-out, there is already every encouragement to do what is deemed appropriate to every local situation. So what do we yet lack? Surely there is every incentive as it is to root the eucharist in the culture and life of the worshippers present?

I offer a combination of the doctrinal and pastoral. A re-touching of the liturgy of the word is discussed in chapter 4 above. But there are three doctrinally sensitive points in the rite, they have pastoral implications, and they can be handled briefly:

(a) Preparation of bread and wine: Rite A rightly does not call this 'Offertory', as the 1662 meaning of that word is an offering of alms.[2] But Rite A does exhibit problems in this area.

Firstly, there is the very odd provision in section 33 for an (unwritten) praise of God 'for his gifts', to which comes the response 'Blessed be God for ever'. In fact, every president of the eucharist who uses it uses it with the Roman Catholic prayers, but that use, which falls within the meaning of the rubrics, is open to very serious criticism: we ought not to be running a mini-Thanksgiving before the major Thanksgiving (lest we anticipate it); we ought not to encourage ourselves to believe that the action of the eucharist is about 'offering' bread and wine; it is probably irrelevant to cite the labour of 'human hands'; and dramatically the sacramental meal is best ushered in with the eucharistic dialogue, clearly designed as the curtain-raiser.[3] 'Laying up' should be without fuss, without liturgical muttering, and without delay.

A secondary (though related) problem is the continued parochial love of 1 Chron. 29 (i.e. section 34—allocated in Rite A to money), which congregations still love to use at this point. We would be better off if it were removed from the main text (perhaps to an appendix of suggestions), and cleaner lines were then left. Very often the text is used when there is no collection of money, though it is quite inappropriate to the sacramental elements.[4] Even when there has been a genuine offering of

[1] Rite B is not in view here.
[2] See my *The End of the Offertory* (Grove Liturgical Study 14, 1978), pp.19-25.
[3] For a fuller discussion see *The End of the Offertory, op. cit.*, p.41.
[4] See *The End of the Offertory*, pp.25-27, 35-37.

alms, it is arguable that a specific mention of it is all out of place between the Peace and the eucharistic action.[1]

(b) The narrative of institution: this needs some handling before we consider the eucharistic prayer. In basic terms, the scriptural text is a kind of 'warrant'. There exists a respectable non-Roman liturgical tradition where the narrative precedes the eucharistic action and both introduces and explains it. First signs exist of Anglicans flirting with the principle. If the narrative does become separate from the eucharistic action then it cannot be narrowly consecratory, and, whereas this point is well made in Rite A, it is not made in this irresistible form, that a eucharistic prayer can exist without the narrative in it—and still the whole prayer is to be reckoned as the liturgical means of consecration. A whole ceremonial rearrangement in turn would stem from an absolute iron-clad case, for currently a significant number of parishes still have genuflexion, ringing of bells, and a general ceremonial spotlighting of the dominical words 'This is my body ... This is my blood'.

(c) The eucharistic prayer: it is clear that old fixed patterns of thinking are over. It may be arguable that there is or should be a broad consistent development of thought within a eucharistic prayer, but we can never now be sent back to the insistence on scholastically precise sets of wording for each part of it.[2] Instead the quest is for simple biblical thanksgivings, preferably responsive, usually joyful in tone, and Christ-centred and salvation-centred on the one hand, but realistic about the unity, life, and mission of the church on the other. The working up of the congregational responses to a rough equality with the presidential monologue element gives both a high sense of participation and a useful level of concentration to the worshippers. There is nothing to be said for turning the presidential parts into a part for two or three or six voices at once. There is much to be said for the home-grown writing of proper prefaces (for those standard eucharistic prayers which can employ them), and for the provision of seasonal and proper whole eucharistic prayers.[3] In addition, it is clear that the Church of England is in many places ready for the improvization of whole chunks of such prayers, though most probably within a given framework, and with known (and cued) congregational responses.

There has, however, been a further cross-current. How far is it biblical or appropriate to invoke the Holy Spirit upon the elements (whether or not upon the worshippers also)? The ASB prayers avoid this, and, at the very least, a full theological debate ought to be joined before those prayers are viewed as too restrictive at this point. The task of the Spirit, if it is to be articulated, ought to relate to the *action* of the rite, and the end-result ought to be in view in such prayers—i.e. not that we should pray that anything should 'happen' to the elements independently of their intended use, terminating on us and our consumption of them.

[1] One fears that it is a love of processing with elements which has attracted the processing with money to this point in the service—and the use of sentences which has then meant the hymn had to be finished (in order that the sentencing could happen) before any laying of the Table occurred.

[2] Thus we are beyond the days of being asked to believe that our Lord intended that we should obey his command 'Do this' by responding with the precise words 'Therefore we offer to you this bread and this cup'. There is no place now for a patristic [1]liturgical verbalistic fundamentalism ... See also the careful advice in the Ecumenical 'Code of Practice'.

[3] The famous 'Lima Liturgy' falls under this heading of a 'proper' eucharistic prayer—i.e. it is for occasions when the Lima Statement, *Baptism, Eucharist and Ministry* is being discussed ecumenically, and it is most certainly not a general Sunday eucharistic work-horse.

I would add two footnotes to the above. One is that there is scope for a much more imaginative range of ways of inviting communicants to participate—extemporary ways, responsive ways, seasonal ways, and praying ways. The other is that the existing provision for supplementary consecration needs purging. The Doctrinal Commission originally advised the Liturgical Commission in 1971 that, if the eucharistic prayer consecrates, then taking more bread and wine and adding it to the existing stock in silence would suffice. The Commission put this in the 'white' Series 3 that year as an alternative, but was driven from it by synodical action. Archbishop Michael Ramsey was tempted from his corner to state that that from which he 'shuddered' with all his being was the thought that the greatest action of God on earth—i.e. eucharistic consecration—should be allowed to happen without the people even knowing it was happening. Even without entering into discussion of whether a supplementary consecration will really bear this doctrinal and devotional weight, we have to recognize that, if my experience around the world is anything to go by, a vast proportion of presidents (and even occasionally other non-presiding presbyters!) take more bread and wine and mutter words—in order not to draw attention to the event, especially if (in a large congregation) administration of communion is still continuing in other parts of the building. This practice lays an axe to the root of Michael Ramsey's principle. If, in addition, the words of institution were excised from the eucharistic prayer itself, and thus could not recur in a form for supplementary consecration, then the end of this liturgical oddity would be in sight.

The post-communion may be worth a mention in its own right. There is a growing use of 'proper' (or at least theme-related) post-communion collects, which can either be supplied as part of a rite, or can derive from private enterprise or *ad hoc* creativity.

Beyond the general provision for eucharistic liturgy—itself perhaps to be supplied 'module-wise'—there are wider eucharistic uses which may utilize these liturgical 'building-blocks' and create different structures from them. There is, for instance, discussion in chapter 6 below concerning the role of intercessions at baptisms, and, in a case like that, once the initiation framework has been established aright, then the eucharistic intercessions can be re-introduced.

The particular and most notable case of the adaptation of the eucharistic rite is the revival of the biblical love-feast (or agape). Here a larger framework than usual must must both give structure to the meal, and give a worshipping content to it, and fit the specifically sacramental material into it.[1]

---

[1] See the provision in *Lent Holy Week Easter,* pp.97-98, and Trevor Lloyd *Celebrating the Agape To-day* (Grove Worship Series no. 97, 1986), and the 1988 Lambeth Statement (MM) paragraph 204, and my commentary on it in *Lambeth and Liturgy 1988,* pp.20-21.

6. BAPTISM AND CONFIRMATION

I think the bones of the liturgical material for baptism and confirmation are right, though with one notable exception. The problems are more usually related to putting the right flesh and blood on the bones—and of providing the right coaching material as pastoral introductions to the separate services.[1] I take issues in sequence through the rites.

Pre-Baptismal Rites

The ASB provides a pair of services for infants; the Roman Catholic Church now has an articulated set of rites for adults; there are often whispers around asking why we cannot enrol infants in a catechumenate.

The existing 'dry run' services for infants do not belong with 'Initiation' at all. They have been welcomed generally, and have proved flexible enough for three uses, almost exclusive:

(i) for parents bringing a child when they have accepted (either voluntarily or through the local church having forced the matter) that the commitment of baptism is not appropriate to where the family stands in relation to God and his church.

(ii) for parents bringing a child when they do not believe that a child is a proper candidate for baptism at all, but do not want simply on those grounds to separate from the Church of England.

(iii) for parents who want to give thanks for the birth (or adoption) of a child as a separate event for the baptism which is going to follow.[2]

There would be far greater pressure for increasing provision in the case of adult baptism. The whole pattern of an adult catechumenate is beginning to fascinate the Church of England. There are models from both antiquity and modern Roman Catholicism. There are other Anglican Provinces which have gone down this route. There is a wealth of materials and a fair degree of Anglican experience to hand. There is, of course, no question of having to stay within any concept of an 'alternative' service.

There is first of all a theological question: should the process of sacramental initiation look primarily to scriptural models (where an immediate and cleancut administration of baptism normally provided the sole means of entry into the life of the church, without catechumenate or probationary period); or should it look to later patristic models where a developed catechumenate preceded baptism); or are we simply to think in terms of pastoral usefulness, without respect to biblical or other precedent? One of the biggest problems in practice is that between seven and nine tenths of adults candidates for confirmation do not need in fact baptism, whilst the

---

[1] I may be unduly conscious of this factor here, simply because I am constantly at such rites in greatly varying surrounds, and with greatly varying planning. But I suspect that the need for help is genuinely there.

[2] Again, this may be either because the parents have desired it that way, or because the local church has formulated a policy whereby baptism is only provided for those who first come for a thanksgiving service. See my *Policies for Infant Baptism* (Grove Worship Series 98, 1987) pp.22-23.

last ten to thirty per cent do, yet for practical purposes both sets are usually channelled together down the same preparation. In purist terms it is difficult to treat the already baptized as catechumens in the true sense of the word, whilst the Roman Catholic models in fact reckon that the process towards baptism (by a series of different liturgical and spiritual formative steps) is clearly for those who are initially seeking baptism.[1]

It would of course be possible for some provision for, e.g. enrolling catechumens publicly, to be provided in connection with baptism without thereby pre-judging what forms of preparation were appropriate in every circumstance, and particularly for when the baptized and unbaptized were being prepared together.

Adult and Household Baptism

There is a major theological problem about the confirmation of those baptized as adults, and I return to that below. But baptism itself could well be embellished from the basic rite in the book. In my judgment, with adults the following elements could, and desirably should, be added to the rite:

(a) a liturgical pattern for sponsors to introduce and present the candidates and undertake nurture after baptism.

(b) provision for candidates to give testimony.[2] Liturgically this may come either in the ministry of the word (which enables the sermon to build upon it) or last thing before baptism, as, e.g., 'Bill, why do you wish to be baptized?'—'Because in the last few months I have come into a living faith in Jesus as Lord'.

(c) when an adult (and an infant) comes from the waters of baptism, it is well worth trying an ejaculatory shout, as, e.g., for the minister to shout out 'Praise God for Bill's baptism into Christ', with a response like 'Hallelujah. Amen.'[3]

(d) the welcome could be not only corporate but also more personal, perhaps with individuals (whether senior members of the congregation or the specific sponsors) saying a personal (but public) word of welcome.

(e) At the moment there exists a real problem re the Welcome—which is intended to include both baptismal and confirmation candidates. It is

[1] See the Roman Catholic 'RCIA', and Anglican adaptation and exposition in books by Peter Ball, in Paul Tudge, *Initiating Adults: Lessons from the Roman Catholic Rite* (Grove Worship Series 102, 1988), and in an essay by Robert Brooks 'The Catechumenate: A Case History' in Thomas Talley (ed.) *A Kingdom of Priests: Liturgical Formation of the People of God* (Alcuin/GROW Joint Liturgical Study 5, Grove Books, 1988) pp.15-19.

[2] This is specifically recommended in the Lambeth 1988 statement (MM) para. 200. If there are large numbers of candidates it becomes difficult for all to do, but can still be done by one or two.

[3] If the signing with the cross is removed from after baptism to an earlier point (which is good sense) there does seem a need of *something* post-baptismal by which the congregation recognizes and acclaims the baptism—a step prior to the 'welcoming' for which provision is already made.

probably needed soon after baptism, and can be accompanied by applause, cheering, or extemporary praise and prayer—or by something not far removed from what we currently have. But it should not then lead on to the confirmation, and, if confirmation is also in the rite, then there should be a different kind of welcome for those confirmed.

(f) The Peace could also be strengthened, perhaps to include reference to the neophytes' admission to communion.

(g) There remains a need for intercession. Some overseas Books (as, e.g. the Canadian *BAS*) have provided place for this within the baptismal rite. Further provision can also be made after communion. I have experience of *extemporary* prayer for the candidates within the baptismal rite, and this can be provided at one of two or three different points.

Confirmation

I have separated this from baptism, as here is where the notable change is needed. We are now reaching the time when the Church of England should take steps to remove the requirement of confirmation following adult baptism. The Liturgical Commission called for a hard look at this question in its introduction in 1977 to the first draft of what are now the ASB Initiation services.[1] The Canadian *Book of Alternative Services* has taken the step and abolished the requirement. The Americans nearly did so further back in the early 1970s, but their bishops lacked the nerve of their Standing Commission—even so, confirmation has been removed from any 'initiation' context in their Book. Can our Commission and House of Bishops grasp the nettle together? Oh yes, and it does not mean that bishops would be marginalized—they could well officiate at adult baptisms, and would still confirm those baptized as infants.

If this development were to be promoted, then baptism (with its welcomes) might well occur at the same (episcopal) rite of confirmation as it does now (with its altered welcomes—see above)—but we would not expect the same persons to be candidates for both.

In other respects the confirmation rite—provided it did not attempt to equate confirmation with the initial gift of the Spirit, could follow its present lines, adapted (e.g. in respect of intercession) as suggested above for baptism.[2]

Children and Communion

At the moment baptism does not admit directly to communion in the Church of England. The very odd liturgical juxtaposition results, whereby,

---

[1] '. . . particularly in the case of adults . . . problems do arise when attempting to justify the confirmation of adults who have just been baptized . . . Some members of the Commission feel that the time has come when this issue must be faced.' (*Initiation Services* (GS 343, SPCK, 1977), p.7).

[2] Providing one set of vows (or declarations) which some affirm for the first time, and others renew, has its clumsinesses, but is probably still neater in most circumstances than having two sets. The oddest issue is the processing down to a West end font of up to 70 candidates for confirmation along with one or two only for the baptism to which they are processing. There *might* be a case for interrogating the confirmation candidates after the baptism was completed.

when an infant is baptized during communion, at the 'Welcome' we say:
'We welcome you . . . as a fellow-member of the body of Christ . . .'
and then at the breaking of bread we say:
'We who are many are one body because we all share in the one bread'
when in fact those admitted to the body in baptism are being excommunicated (in fact ex-corporated) minutes later. Apparently we await the response of the dioceses to *Children in the Way* before General Synod will pick up this issue.[1] I can only plead that the matter is very urgent if Christian family units are to function *as* one in Christ with each other in the growing secularist, superstitious, and pluralist religious climate in which we in England live. The liturgical implications of this change would be to link baptismal and eucharistic rites more closely—and to relieve confirmation of any implication that it was admitting to communion.[2]

In passing we may also note that the desire for 'eucharistic prayers for use with children' has up till now been staved off simply because young children were not communicant, and it seems perverse to write liturgy for those who are strictly marginalized by its own provisions. If this change now came, it could well give a liberty of writing eucharistic texts which, one might hope, would not be solely for young children, but at least had a more inclusive all-age look to them.

Other Initiation-linked Rites

In the USA and Canada, there are rites like confirmation (but differing) both for renewal of baptismal vows on other occasions, and for reception from other denominations. Both are immediate needs in the Church of England. My personal hope would be that the 'renewal' issue would find the Commission and the House of Bishops ready to recognize the understandable desire among many for the swamping or submersion offered in baptism, when in fact they received something more sparing of the water in infant baptism. I believe we ought to be ready to meet this request with a dignified liturgical rite, distinguishable from baptism by submersion as follows: by the preparation for it, by the confession by the candidate at it of already being baptized, by the rest of the liturgical text, by preaching, and by the registration or certifying of the event. With that fivefold wall around the ducking, I really cannot see how people can yet go on objecting 'Oh, people will still confuse it with baptism'. That is not my experience, and I speak from experience.[3]

[1] The general procedural position is this: the Knaresborough report *Communion before Confirmation?* (Church House Publishing, 1985) was debated once in General Synod and deposited with the House of Bishops, which, from a question and answer in General Synod in November 1988, apparently declines to consider it further except in connection with *Children in the Way,* concerning which dioceses have to respond to General Synod by 1 January 1990. That report simply says the matter is urgent (p.52) and that the arguments are to be found in the Knaresborough report. Dioceses would be wise, when debating *Children in the Way,* to pass motions about this issue, and send them in to General Synod, or the issue will be lost from sight. (On a wider front, the first intentional Anglican Liturgical Consultation at Boston, Mass., in July 1985 published a 'Boston Statement' calling for admission of young children to communion on the basis of their baptism, and, whilst the ACC-7 report in 1987 questioned this, the issue was also the subject of a unanimous Resolution 69 at the Lambeth Conference—cf. *Lambeth and Liturgy 1988,* pp.16-17 and 24-25).
[2] See my *Anglican Confirmation* (Grove Liturgical Study 48, 1986) p.48.
[3] See also the 1988 Lambeth Statement (MM) para. 201 and my commentary on it in *Lambeth and Liturgy 1988* p.21.

7. OTHER RITES

Marriage

The future of the marriage rite is bound up with two main questions: how does the Church of England view the marriage of divorcees? And: should the normal context for getting married be a church wedding? Both have some liturgical implications—for there are desires for some expression of penitence to be incorporated in the marriage of divorcees, and, if the Church of England does not provide a full marriage rite, then the pattern of church provision will begin to follow *Prayer and Dedication after a Civil Marriage,* rather than the marriage rite we currently have.

In general, the ASB rite has been well received. There are verbal infelicities (e.g. the bathos of 'after serious thought' in the Preface, and the mysterious 'worship' in the asymmetrical form of the vows); it is still arguable that the permission for the ministry of the word before the marriage does not actually help people to *pray* for the couple; and in the offing are questions based on the RCIA as to whether 'initiation' into matrimony also might not have a series of liturgical steps, as, on this pattern, does baptism. The marriage of the divorced and the widowed raises a question as to the part of the children of one or other partner in the rite; and the frequency of pre-marital co-habitation raises questions about how (or whether) this is taken into account in the rite—and also as to whether the children who are the fruit of the actual liaison have any part also.[1]

Funerals

That which was one rite in Cranmer's day is becoming diversified, and the ASB provision itself does not always meet the need (witness the new Commission's provision of a rite for peri-natal purposes). The minimal order, for use in a 10-12 minute event in the crematorium chapel, proves to be barely more than a scripture sentence, prayer, reading, brief word, Lord's prayer and one or two other prayers, commendation and committal, blessing—and out. It hardly needs any official text at all, and is usually not followed in a book by the mourners. On the other hand, a Christian congregation in a church building may well expect and deserve far more. The need is for structures, module-type 'propers', and an underlying theology.

There is no denying the ignorance of Christianity and of the resurrection of Jesus Christ in a vast proportion of current funerals which are nominally Christian. The Commission of twenty years ago faced this in the early seventies, and vowed to keep the Christian character of the rite as full-blooded and scriptural as possible. The secular pressures since then have been enormous—and there are, of course, nowadays also 'mixed' funerals, where, for instance, the dead wife was Christian, but the widower and all his family are Sikhs. I would hope that the secular and pluralist pressures would not lead us far into losing our confidence in Christ as *the* hope of life eternal.

---

[1] We go beyond liturgy if we follow this too far. But experience suggests that the competitive costs of the sub-culture of weddings—and the need to outdo the Joneses—has often in England to-day caused a corner-cutting into (stable) co-habitation simply on economic grounds. If so, the clergy have some duty to keep expectations of the subculture down, and thus help avoid the consumerist spiral.